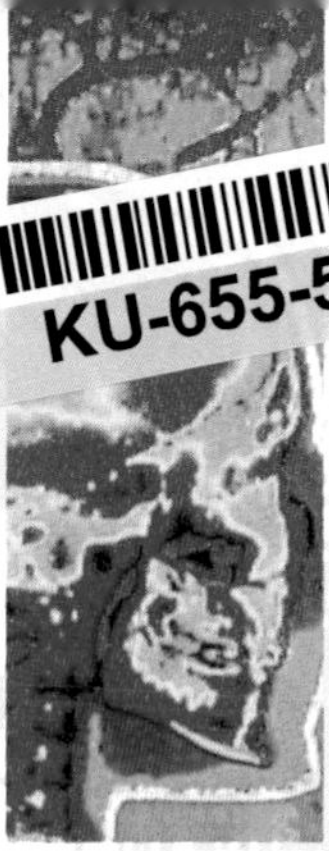

SCIENCE QUEST

TIME

ROBERT SNEDDEN

Belitha Press

This edition published in 2003 by
Belitha Press
A member of Chrysalis Books plc
64 Brewery Road, London, N7 9NT

Picture acknowledgements
Ancient Art and Architecture Collection: 13 (bottom left).
Collections: 38 (top) Anthea Sieveking.
Mary Evans Picture Library: 4-5 (top) Explorer, 13 (bottom right), 14, 43.
Ronald Grant Archive: 6 (bottom).
Robert Harding Picture Library: 38 (bottom).
Michael Holford: 12 (top left).
Image Select: 25 (bottom) Ann Ronan Picture Library.
Mansell Collection: 9 (bottom), 17.
Oxford Scientific Films: 7 (top, all) Avril Ramage, 8 (all) Tim Shepherd.
Science Photo Library: 9 (centre) Robin Scagill, 10 (top) Gordon Garradd, 16 NASA, 18 (left) Dr Jeremy Burgess, 25 (top left and top right), 26 (top) J-L Charmet, 28 Alexander Tsiaras, 34-35 NASA, 37, 41 Kent Wood.
Tony Stone Worldwide: 26 (bottom).
Syndication International: 42.
John Walmsley: 5 (centre and bottom).
Zefa: 7 (bottom).

ISBN 1 84138 497 6

Printed in China by Imago

British Library Cataloguing in Publication Data
CIP data for this book is available from the British Library.

Editor: Neil Champion
Designer: John Calvert
Consultant: Professor Christopher Isham
Picture research: Juliet Duff
Cover illustration: Oliver Burston
Other illustrations: David Pugh

contents

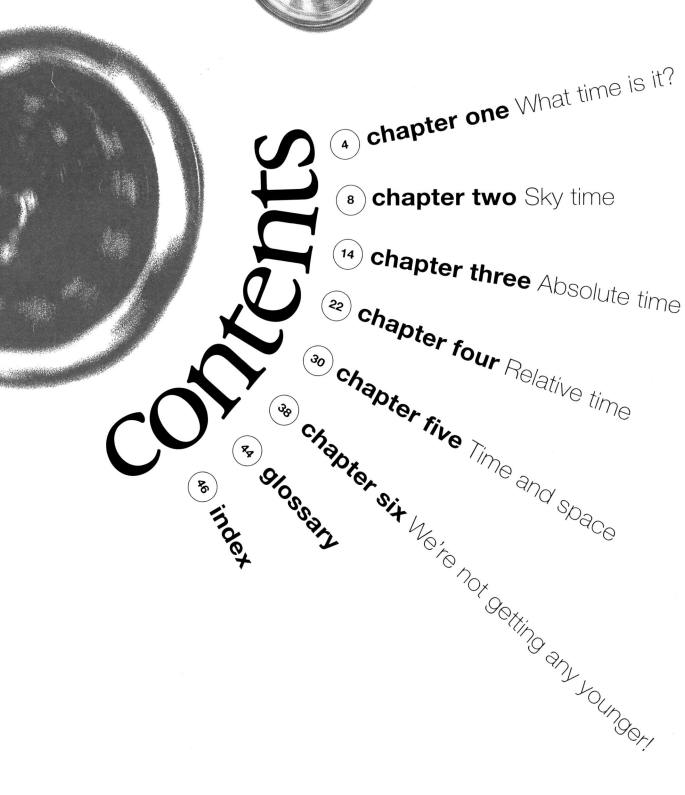

CHAPTER ONE

What time is it?

Probably the first thing you do when you wake up in the morning is to wonder what the time is. But have you ever wondered what time is?

Take a look at your watch or at a clock. What does it tell you? You might answer that it tells you the time – eight o'clock, half past eleven, quarter to four, whatever it happens to be. If you have a digital watch you might say that the time is 0800, 1130 or 1545. What is it that these numbers are telling you? Perhaps that it will soon be time to go to school, or time to have lunch, or time to watch your favourite TV programme, or time to go home.

It takes time

Knowing what the time is can be very useful. We use time to keep our lives in order – it lets us know when to do things, or when something will happen. If you say to someone, 'I'll meet you at five o'clock,' they will know when to expect you. If you want to watch a television programme you can look in a newspaper to find out what time it is on. Then you won't miss it. You can look in a timetable to find out when a train will arrive (if it is on time). Everything takes time.

We can split time up into as many different bits as we want to. People who study history may look at events that happened hundreds of years ago. Photographers can set their cameras to take pictures in less than a thousandth of a second.

We have watches and clocks to measure minutes and hours. Many people keep diaries to remind them of what is happening from day to day. We also have calendars which measure weeks

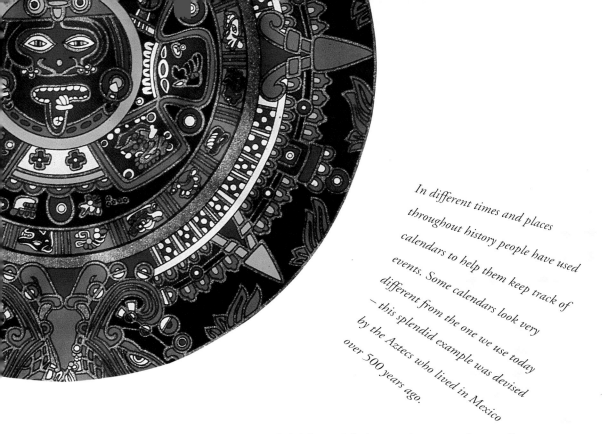

In different times and places throughout history people have used calendars to help them keep track of events. Some calendars look very different from the one we use today – this splendid example was devised by the Aztecs who lived in Mexico over 500 years ago.

and months and give us useful bits of information, such as the dates of people's birthdays and holidays.

What's the time?

People weren't always so concerned about keeping a close watch on time. They relied on events in the world around them, such as the rising of the Sun or the coming of winter, to order their lives. They weren't really very bothered about unimportant things such as knowing how old they were. The invention of the clock changed people's lives completely. They became more aware of time. They started to worry about time passing. They wanted to save time.

What is it that is so special about time? It doesn't seem to be like anything else. Often you will hear people talking about time as if it were something that had a length. 'That took a long time,' they might say. Sometimes you might hear someone say, 'Time hangs heavy on my hands,' as though time had weight. You can take a ruler and measure the length of this book and it will always be the same length. You can put it on some scales and weigh it and it will always be the same weight. But how do you measure something you can't see or feel, like time?

Sometimes it seems that you can't rely on your watch to tell how much time has passed. How long do you mean when you talk about a long time? When you are happy and enjoying what

Have you noticed how time often appears to go at different speeds? If you are doing something that is fun, time seems to fly by, but doing something that is boring can take forever!

you are doing, time seems to fly past. If you are bored, time seems to pass slowly. Yet a book will always be the same length whatever mood you are in!

Writers of fiction have often played around with the idea of travelling in time. The Back to the Future *series of films was one example of this, but scientists are still undecided as to whether or not time travel might really be possible.*

Where does the time go?

Whenever you do something you have to use a different piece of time. You can't reuse time as you can a ruler or a book. You may be able to run a race in 20 seconds, but every time you do it you use a different 20 seconds. The time you use has gone forever and you can never get it back. If you could use the same time again and again you would never get any older. Imagine if time was like distance and you could walk back to your sixth birthday!

Time seems only to go in one direction. You would think it very strange if your watch started to run backwards, or plants grew back into the ground, or a broken plate mended itself.

When did it happen?

So there are things we can do with time and there are ways we can measure it. But we still don't know what it is. What do all those bits of time – seconds, hours, years – actually mean? If you say to someone, 'I'll meet you in an hour,' what are you really saying? You mean that you'll be there when the minute-hand on your watch has gone right round once, because that is what an hour is. But an hour can be other things as well. It can be the time it takes for a fast train to go 160 kilometres or your heart to beat about 4,500 times. What you are really saying is that something happens and it takes what we call an hour.

If nothing happened anywhere, would time still pass? How could you possibly know that it had? Many people have wondered if there would be any time at all if absolutely nothing was happening anywhere. Perhaps time is just things happening and can't exist on its own.

We only see time going one way – into the future. It would appear very odd indeed if a rotten apple suddenly became fresh again.

You may think you have a good idea of what time is all about, but the world of time can be a strange one. Some people think that time can run backwards, and that it may be possible, although very difficult, to travel in time. Perhaps after you read this book you will begin to see that the apparently simple question, 'What time is it?' isn't so easy to answer after all.

High speed photography allows us to see events that last only a fraction of a second. It is difficult to imagine a length of time so short that nothing could happen.

CHAPTER TWO

Sky time

It is difficult enough to try and say what we mean by time. But what did people who lived thousands of years ago think about time? Almost certainly, they didn't think of it in the way that we do.

These days we are used to splitting time up into different lengths – seconds, days, years – to suit different purposes. But people didn't always divide time like this. There was no need to tell the time with great accuracy when there were no aeroplanes to catch, no television programmes to remember to watch, no set time to be at school or to arrive at work.

Before there were clocks and watches people relied on natural, regularly repeated events, such as the changing seasons, to keep track of time.

People relied on natural events to measure the passing of time. They wanted to know when to plant or harvest their crops, or when the hunting would be good, or when to find shelter for the night. The exact day, or minute didn't matter. Many of the peoples who lived in the northern part of the world reckoned years by counting winters. Winter was a quiet period when preparations were made for the coming spring planting season, so it was a good time to choose to mark each year's passing.

The solar year

One way to keep track of the changing year is by watching the Sun. It appears lower in the sky in winter than in summer. In summer it is in the sky longer and so there is more daylight. People could keep track of the changing seasons by the amount of daylight. They realized that the Sun rose in different places as the year progressed. A year had passed when the Sun rose in the same place again. This is called a **solar year**. What actually happens is that the Earth moves, not the Sun. One year is the time the Earth takes to go round, or orbit, the Sun. Some people built huge temples of wood and stone columns that showed where the Sun would rise on the longest and shortest days, or the days that summer returned or the harvest started.

For centuries the Sun was worshipped by peoples all over the world. It was the source of light and warmth, and also the great natural timekeeper. Temples such as Stonehenge were constructed to show where it would rise at different times of the year.

Sun worshipping was a common religious event in many ancient societies. People thought that the Sun went round the Earth, but the Polish astronomer, Copernicus, proved this to be wrong.

During the course of a night the stars in the sky appear to rotate around a single point. People used to believe that the stars were fixed to a huge bowl, called the celestial sphere, that turned around above the Earth.

Stonehenge, in England, is a well-known example of one of these giant clocks. It was built over 3,000 years ago.

Night and day

As it travels around the Sun, the Earth is also spinning round on its axis and it is this that makes it look as if the Sun and Moon rise in the east and move across the sky to set in the west. A day is the time between one sunrise and another, or between one sunset and another. The rising and setting of the Sun told people when a new day was beginning.

The ancient Egyptians and Greeks both chose sunrise as the start of the new day, but other peoples, such as the Jews and the Muslims, chose sunset. Today, we also use the word day to mean just that part of a whole day when the Sun is in the sky.

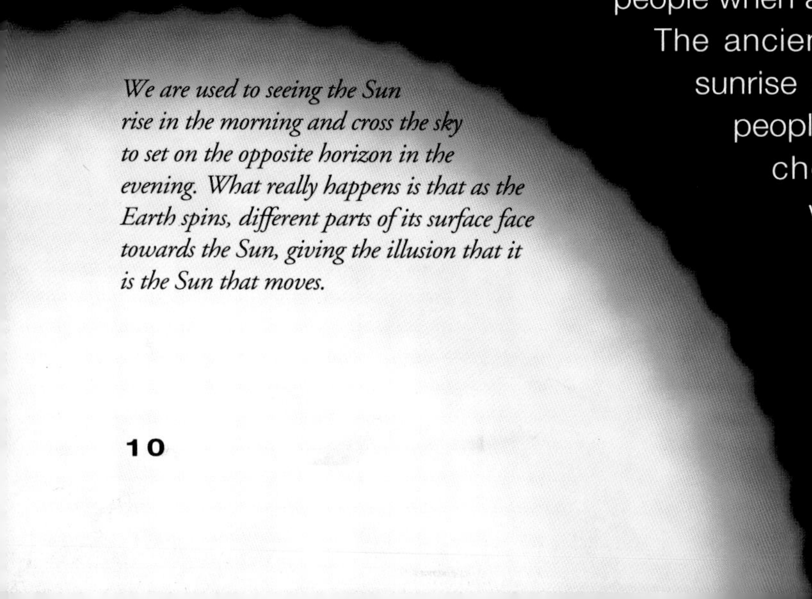

We are used to seeing the Sun rise in the morning and cross the sky to set on the opposite horizon in the evening. What really happens is that as the Earth spins, different parts of its surface face towards the Sun, giving the illusion that it is the Sun that moves.

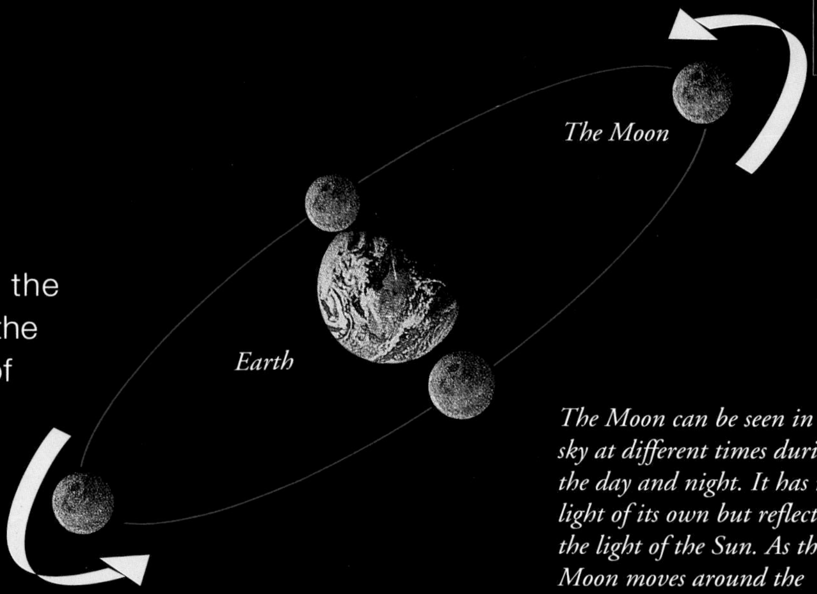

The Moon can be seen in the sky at different times during the day and night. It has no light of its own but reflects the light of the Sun. As the Moon moves around the Earth in its circular orbit it always keeps the same side facing the Earth.

Another way of measuring the length of a day is to call it the time between each arrival of the Sun at its highest point in the sky. This is known as a **solar day**.

You need to remember that it is because the Earth spins that the Sun appears to cross the sky. A day is really the time it takes for the Earth to spin completely round its axis once.

The hours of darkness

It was the Egyptians who decided to divide up a day into 24 hours. They didn't start by dividing up the daylight hours, however. Instead they started with the night. By carefully studying the movements of the stars in the night sky they realized that they could divide up the night.

The regular motion of the stars across the night sky makes them excellent natural clocks. Just like the movement of the Sun during the day, this apparent movement of the stars across the night sky is also caused by the Earth spinning.

A day can be measured as the length of time it takes for the stars to make one complete turn. A day measured in this way is called a **sidereal day**. This word comes from a Latin word meaning 'star'. A sidereal day is actually about four minutes shorter than a solar day.

The Egyptians decided to divide the night into 12 parts or hours. The start of each part was marked by the rising of a particular star or group of stars above the eastern horizon. For the sake of balance they thought that there should also be the same number of daylight hours. This is why we now have a day that is 24 hours long.

As the position of the Sun in the sky changes, the shadows it casts change position too. A sundial can be used to tell the time by the position of the shadow cast by its gnomon (the upright part) at different times of the day.

The Egyptians needed a way to divide up the daylight hours. They used the Sun to do this by using a sundial – the oldest one that has been found is more than 3,500 years old. As the Sun moves across the sky, the shadows it casts move as well. A sundial has an upright part called a **gnomon** that casts a shadow across a surface that is marked into 12 equal sections. Each section represents an hour, matching the 12 hours of the night. Gnomon means 'one who knows' – it can tell you what the time is by the movement of the shadow on the dial.

The Moon and the month

As well as being able to measure a day and a year it is useful to have something in between. The Moon goes through regular phases, from full moon to new moon (when the Moon is not visible in the sky) and back to full again. This happens as the Moon travels round the Earth and the angle of the Sun's rays reflecting from it changes. The time between one full moon and the next is called a month. A month, therefore, is the time the Moon takes to go round the Earth once.

The calendar

Problems arose when people tried to put these different ways of measuring time together to keep a record of the changing year called a calendar. For instance, a **lunar month** is actually just over 29½ days, and there aren't an exact number of lunar months in a solar year. In fact, there are 12 lunar months and 11 days in a solar year. (If you do the sum you'll see that makes 365 days.)

To complicate things still further, there aren't an exact number of days in a year, because the Earth spins around 365¼ times as it goes around the Sun once.

All this means that making calendars that work is an awkward business. The Babylonians, who lived in what is now Iraq, used the lunar month as the basis of their calendar. They added an extra month every now and again to make up a year as reckoned

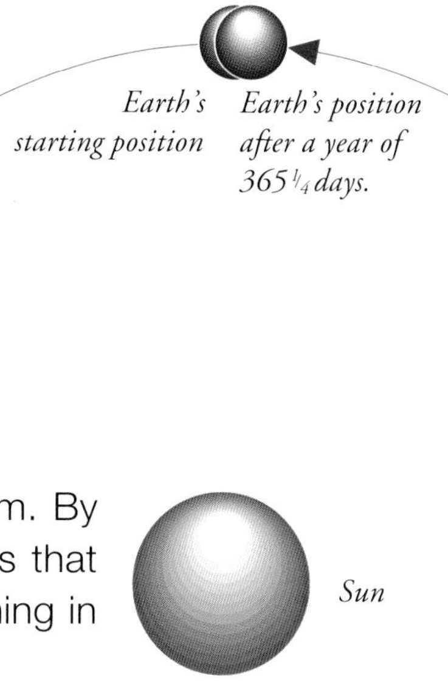

by the Sun. The Greeks and Romans used a similar system. By the time of Julius Caesar, the calendar was in such a mess that the months that used to fall in the winter were now happening in the autumn.

In 46 BC, Julius Caesar, acting on the advice of the Greek astronomer Sosigenes, made a new calendar based on a year that was 365¼ days long. This was a little longer than the actual solar year and as time went on the calendar became more and more inaccurate.

The modern calendar

With the help of an astronomer called Sosigenes, Caesar tried to sort things out by making the year 45 BC 445 days long. This was called the year of confusion. Since that time a year has been 365 days long. Caesar also introduced the **leap year**. This was necessary because a year doesn't divide up into an exact number of days, so every fourth year an extra day was added to the month of February.

Unfortunately, Caesar and Sosigenes were a little bit out in their calculations. Their year of 365¼ days was actually longer than the solar year by 11 minutes and 14 seconds. This meant that the calendar became a day out every 128 years. By the time of Pope Gregory XIII, more than 1600 years later, the calendar was wrong by ten days.

Pope Gregory introduced a completely new calendar in 1582. In that year he announced that the day after 4 October would not be 5 October, but 15 October. It was also decided there would be only 97 leap years in every 400 years, rather than 100. So only century years that could be divided by 400 (such as the year 2000) would be leap years. This resolved the problem of that awkward extra 11 minutes. This calendar is called the **Gregorian calendar**, after Pope Gregory, and is now used throughout the world.

By the sixteenth century astronomers could measure the length of a year quite accurately. Using this information Pope Gregory XIII reformed the calendar again. The changes he made meant that ten days had to be dropped from one year. People feared they were losing these days from their lives.

CHAPTER THREE

Absolute time

Around the time that Pope Gregory XIII's new calendar was introduced, Galileo Galilei made a discovery that would prove to be of great importance in the history of time measurement.

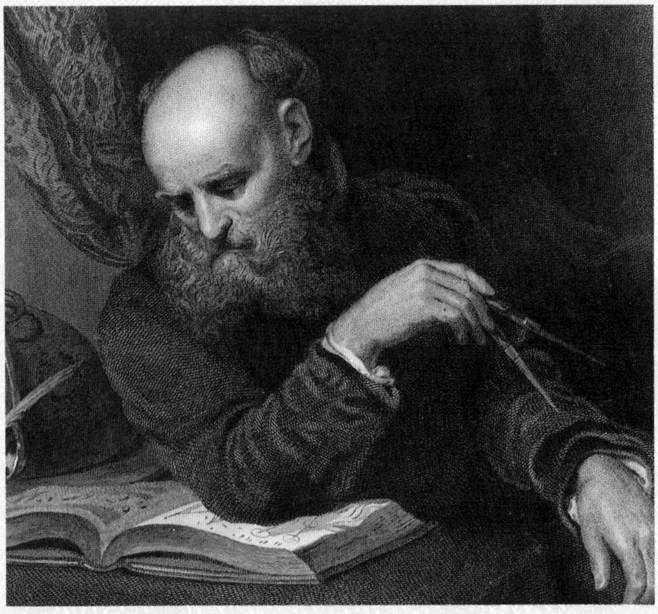

During a boring sermon in the cathedral of Pisa, in Italy, Galileo watched a huge **chandelier** swinging gently from side to side. Using his pulse as a clock, he timed the swings. He was surprised to discover that whether the swings were long or short they always took the same amount of time.

The swinging pendulum

Galileo didn't write about his discovery until 1602, about 20 years later. He established that a pendulum, the name given to a freely-swinging weight suspended from a point, always behaved in a certain way. It doesn't matter how heavy the pendulum is, or how far it swings, it always takes the same length of time to go back and forth once. In fact, the length of time it takes for the pendulum to swing depends only on the length of the pendulum. This means that it is very easy to change the time each swing takes. You simply lengthen or shorten the pendulum. The pendulum does just what you want a clock to do. That is, it does

It takes the same amount of time for both these pendulums to complete one swing.

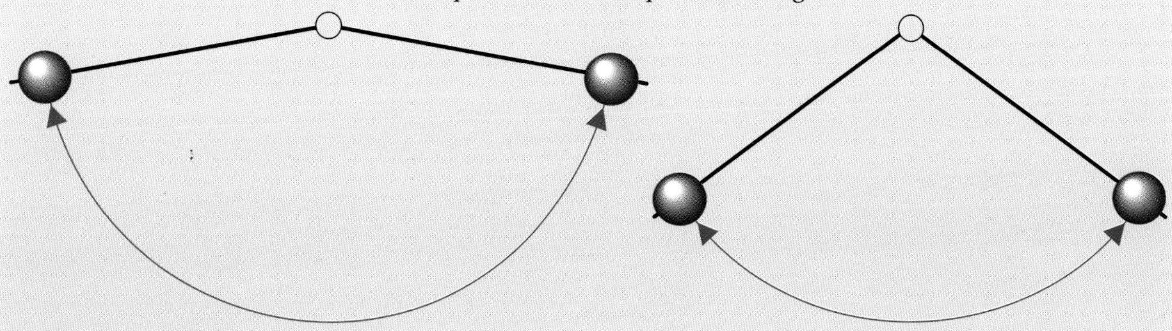

Through careful observation, Galileo discovered that a pendulum always takes the same time to complete one swing no matter how far you push it. Increasing or decreasing the weight on the end of the pendulum doesn't change the time of the swing either. The only way to make the pendulum take a longer or shorter time for each swing is to change its length.

You can try this for yourself by making pendulums using different lengths of string with different weights tied to the end. Try experimenting to see what results you get. Two pendulums of the same length but with different weights should keep in step with each other. In 1656 Christiaan Huygens used Galileo's discovery to make the first pendulum clock.

the same thing over and over again, reliably and regularly so that you can use it to measure how long it takes for other events to happen. It might take 20 swings of the pendulum to run 100 metres, for instance.

Several years later Galileo described how a pendulum might be used to make a clock that kept good time. He produced designs for a pendulum clock, but none was made. It wasn't until 15 years after his death that the Dutch scientist Christiaan Huygens made the first working pendulum clock.

The speedometer on a car shows how fast it is travelling – 60 km/h means that in one hour it will travel 60 kilometres.

Time and motion

Galileo was aware of the importance of being able to measure time when carrying out scientific experiments. He wanted to work out what made objects move the way they did, but to do this he had to be able to time them accurately. You can only know how fast an object is travelling if you know how much time it takes to travel from one point to another. This makes a good way of measuring time essential. As he had no mechanical clocks, Galileo had to use his pulse and **water clocks**. He also had to make sure that his objects kept moving long enough for him to be able to time them.

One of the moons of Jupiter photographed by a Voyager space probe. Galileo was the first person to see Jupiter's moons using the new invention of the telescope.

A new sky clock

Galileo suggested another way of keeping time that involved objects in space. Navigators on board ships needed to know what the time was in order to plot their positions accurately. As no one had succeeded in inventing a clock that worked reliably, other methods of determining the time had to be used.

Galileo, using the new invention of the telescope, discovered that the planet Jupiter had four moons of its own. We now know that there are many more, but Galileo's telescope was not powerful enough to reveal them all. Within a few weeks he had worked out that they followed regular paths around Jupiter. He realized that this reliable source of repeated actions would make an excellent clock. He set about drawing up tables of these moons' movements that could be taken on board ships. It was a good idea, but it didn't work in practice as the movement of a ship made it impossible to use a powerful enough telescope.

Using natural cycles

Galileo helped to change our ideas about time. He saw that if you take natural cycles, such as the phases of the Moon or the Sun rising, as measures of time, you have to decide which one is the **master cycle**, against which you measure all the others. Galileo saw time as something that existed apart from the natural events that were used to measure it.

Perhaps Galileo asked himself the question that we are trying to answer: 'What is it I measure when I measure time?'

Time and motion

Isaac Barrow taught the great scientist Isaac Newton at Cambridge. Barrow thought that mathematicians who used time in their calculations ought to have some idea of what time was. He believed that time keeps going whether we are aware of it or not. He also said that time can only be measured by referring to something else. At the beginning of the book we said that an hour could be the time it takes for the hand on your watch to go round once, or the time it takes for your heart to beat 4,500

Trinity College, Cambridge, where Newton studied.

times. But what time is it? Is it one hour or 4,500 heartbeats? Which one is the master cycle?

Absolute time

Isaac Newton

Isaac Newton was no doubt influenced by Isaac Barrow's ideas. He thought that our usual measurements of time – such as the hour, the day, the month, the year – were all simply **common time**.

These were useful ways of measuring how long something took, but they were not to be confused with true time. Newton called this true time **absolute time**. Absolute time, he said, was completely separate from space and independent of events. It keeps going at the same rate, everywhere in the Universe, whatever is happening. One second for me should be exactly the same length as one second for you, whatever we are doing and wherever we are.

Of course, the trouble with this idea is that we have to use real events to give us some practical idea of time passing. Perhaps we could never measure absolute time directly, but only common time.

Newton himself failed to give a proper definition of time. Saying that time is 'absolute' still doesn't tell you what it actually is. This didn't prevent Newton from using time in his mathematics and his study of movement. In the study of motion he carried on from where Galileo had left off. He turned his findings into three laws, called the laws of motion.

Using these three laws, he was able to explain how all objects move the way they do, including a ball moving through the air, or the planets moving round the Sun. Then he went on to show that his laws of motion were governed by another law that explained how the force of gravity held everything together. He revolutionized the way people looked at the Universe. Newton, it seemed, could explain how the whole Universe moved with just four simple laws.

Newton's absolute time was the unvarying background against which all events took place. He thought that all our measurements of time were just reflections of the great ocean of absolute time.

A challenge to Newton

Newton's laws were unchallenged for 200 years. For everyday purposes they are still an excellent way of describing how things move. Space scientists can use Newton's laws to plot the path of a spacecraft from Earth to Jupiter. But Newton had not explained the cause of the force of gravity. In 1905, Albert Einstein completely demolished the idea of absolute time and put forward an idea that might explain what caused gravity. He also showed that moving objects didn't just indicate the passing of time, they actually slowed time down!

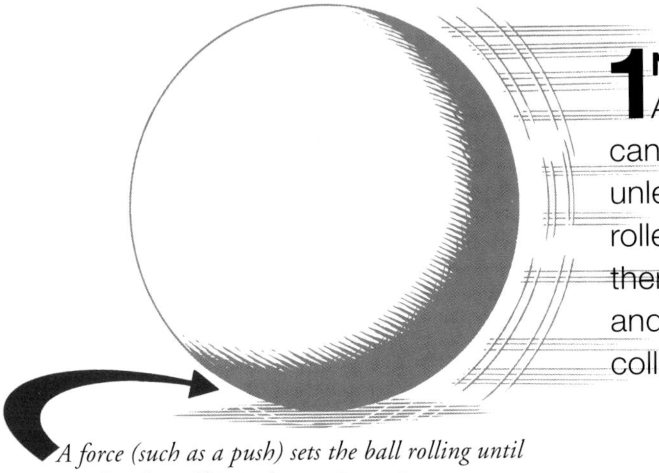

A force (such as a push) sets the ball rolling until another force (friction) stops it moving.

1 Newton's first law of motion

All objects move at the same speed (which can be zero speed) and in the same direction unless acted on by a force. For example, a ball rolled along the ground might roll forever if there were no forces of friction to slow it down and stop it, or if there was nothing for it to collide with.

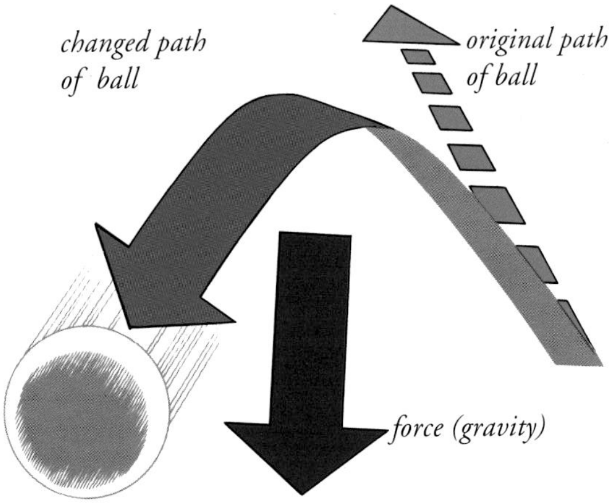

2 Newton's second law of motion

A force acting on an object will cause it to move in the direction of that force. The change of motion depends on the size of the force involved and the mass of the object. A ball flying through the air changes direction and moves in a curve, not a straight line, because the force of gravity attracts it towards the Earth.

3 Newton's third law of motion

If one object exerts a force on another, there is an equal and opposite force, called a reaction, exerted by the second object on the first. Even though the force of your weight is acting downwards towards the ground you can still stand because there is an equal force acting from the ground up. This is why it doesn't feel as though you are being pulled towards the ground all the time.

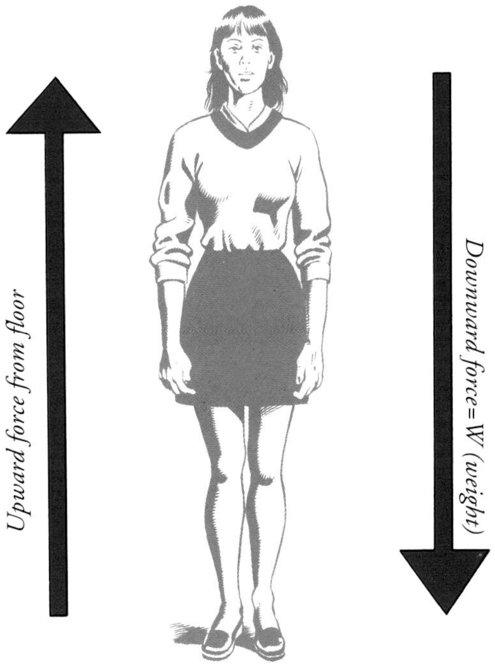

Newton's law of gravitation

Between any two objects there is always a **gravitational force** that attracts the objects to each other. This force acts along a line joining the centres of the two objects. The strength of the force depends on the mass of the objects and on the distance between them. If you double the distance between the two objects, the force of attraction between them becomes a quarter of what it was. If you treble the distance, the force is reduced to a ninth.

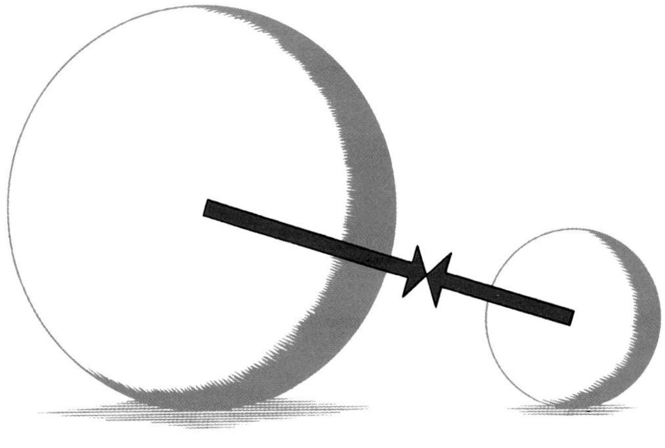

The force of gravity acting between two objects.

CHAPTER FOUR

• Relative time

Newton thought that perhaps there was an absolute space, a sort of three dimensional grid against which all the objects in the Universe could be mapped.

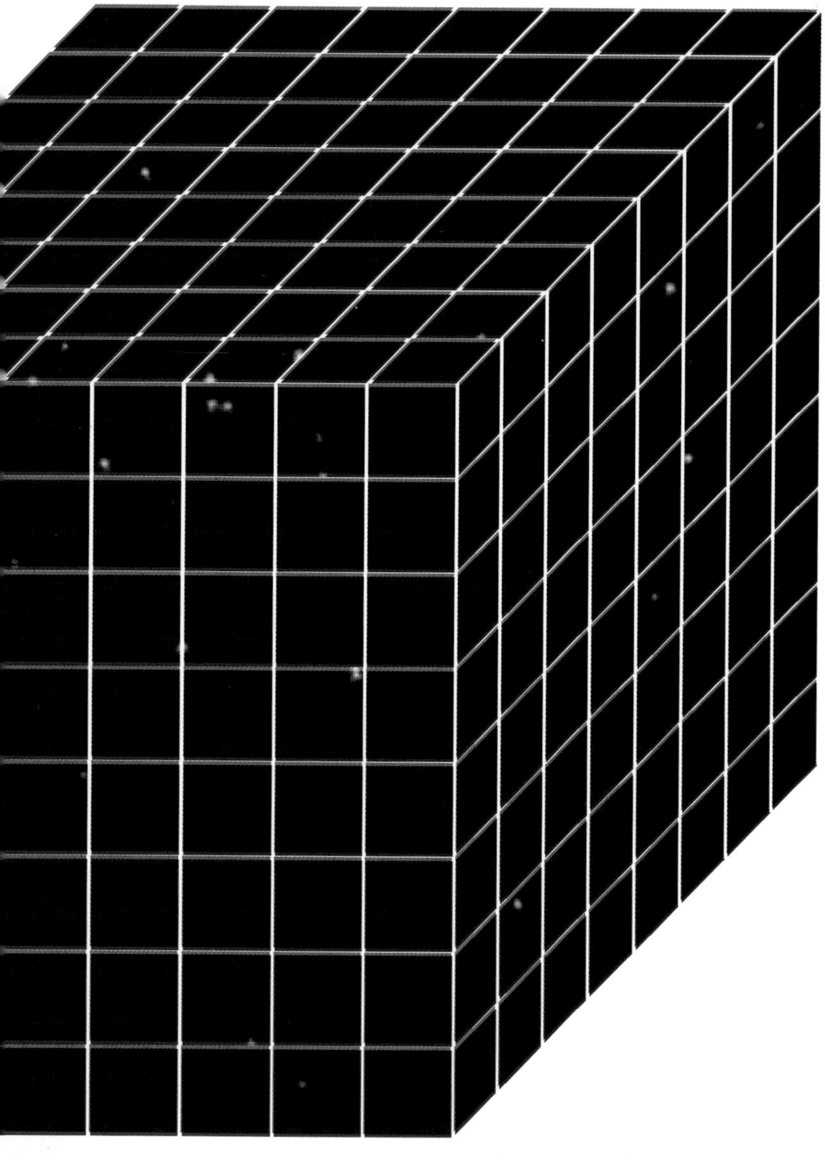

Isaac Newton's idea of absolute time meant that the point in time we call 'now' is the same throughout the Universe. This follows from the notion that time flows at the same rate for everybody, wherever they are. Newton thought that no one could go faster or slower through time than anyone else, so everyone must be at the same moment 'now'.

Newton also believed in the idea of **absolute space**, through which everything moved. Absolute space was the background against which everything happened. He thought that it should be possible to state the **absolute position** of an object in absolute space.

It was as if you could take a giant sheet of graph paper which covered the entire Universe and plot the positions of everything in it. But it is just as impossible to say what absolute space is as it is to define absolute time.

You can only say where something is in relation to other objects. For example, the knight is on a white square next to the bishop on the chessboard. But where is the chessboard?

Because everything in the Universe is moving, you can't say absolutely where something is. You can only give an object a position relative to something else. For instance, I am 50 centimetres from my table – and also about 150 million kilometres from the Sun.

Most scientists accepted Newton's idea of absolute space, although there were problems with it. But they had a major difficulty with light. Experiments showed that light seemed to behave like a wave. If it was a wave, it needed something to travel through. How could light cross the emptiness of absolute space?

The answer that scientists came up with was **aether**. This was a strange, invisible substance that filled absolute space. The scientists thought that light moved through the aether in the same way as sound waves move through the air.

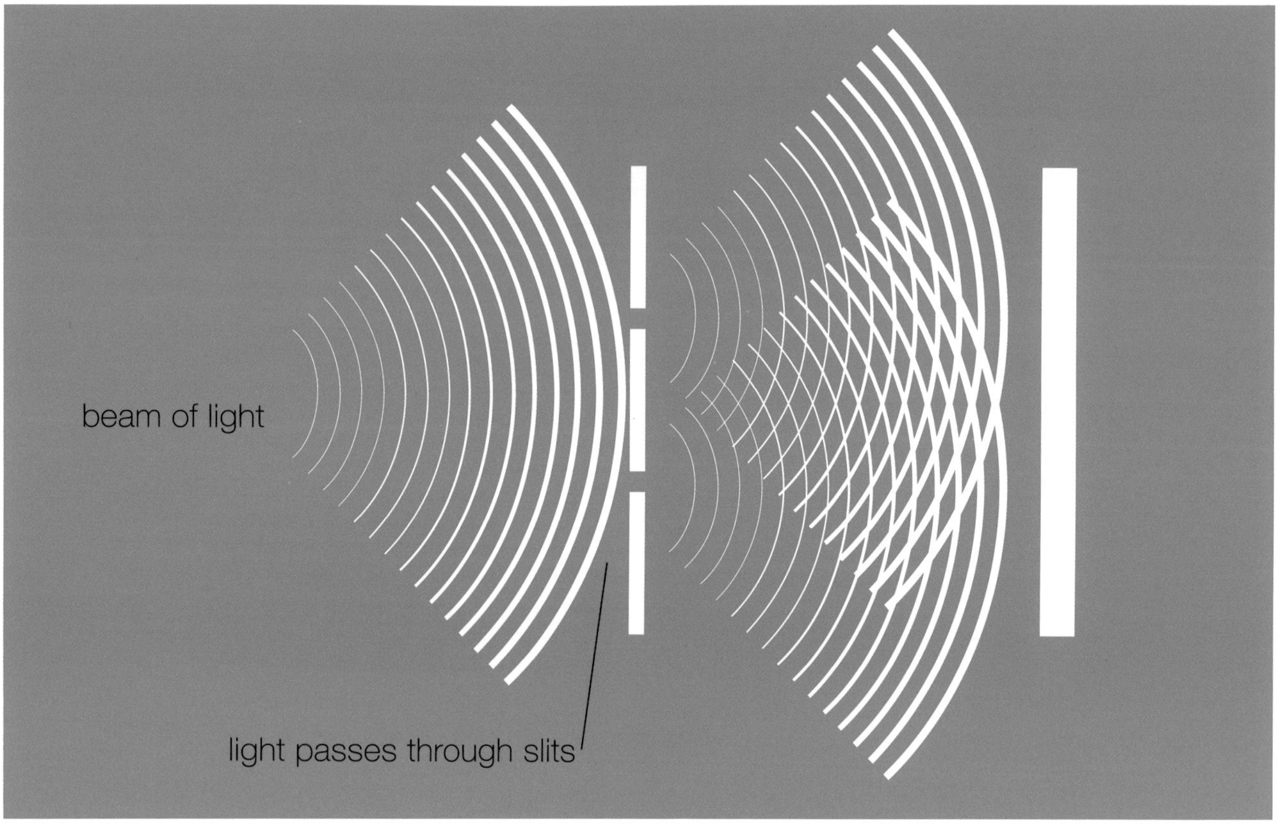

An understanding of the nature of light became of great importance in understanding the nature of time. For centuries people had argued about whether light was a stream of tiny particles, or whether it was a series of waves. Isaac Newton and others favoured the particle theory and for around 200 years this idea had the greatest support. But experiments were carried out that seemed to show that light was, in fact, a form of wave. Beams of light passed through tiny slits would set up ***patterns of interference*** *(as the diagram above shows). This could only be explained by considering light as a wave. Particles just wouldn't behave that way. Waves, of course, needed something to travel through, and this was the reason why scientists put forward the idea of the aether that supposedly filled space. Then two American scientists called Michelson and Morley demonstrated in a famous experiment that there was no aether at all (see next page). Later Albert Einstein came up with a theory that explained their results. Einstein's theory showed that, because the speed of light was* ***constant****, it had an effect on time. But the story of light doesn't end there. Albert Einstein also demonstrated that light really did act like a stream of particles. Light was, amazingly, both wave and particle. It behaves like a wave in some experiments, and like a particle in others.*

The Michelson-Morley experiment

In 1887 two American scientists called Albert Michelson (left) and Edward Morley (right) carried out a famous experiment to demonstrate the existence of aether. People thought that the Earth made an 'aether wind' as it travelled round the Sun. The speed at which a beam of light travelled, varied according to whether it was going with or against the aether wind. Michelson and Morley discovered that it didn't matter how you measured the speed of light, the answer was always the same. The light always travelled at just under 300,000 km per second. The speed didn't change, even if the source of the light beam or the person doing the measuring was moving. This result has since been confirmed by other experiments. It seemed that there was no aether after all.

Scientists tried to come up with explanations, including some that sounded very bizarre, for this result. Some suggested that the Earth dragged the aether around with it so there was no wind. Others thought that objects shrank as they moved through

Albert Michelson's interferometer, a machine he invented to measure the speed of light.

Albert Einstein

the aether. Or the reason that the speed of light seemed to be the same in all directions was that the equipment the scientists used to measure the speed had changed size.

Special relativity

Then in 1905 Albert Einstein published a much better explanation of the way the Universe worked. He put forward two new ideas. First, that the laws of physics, the set of rules that say how the Universe works, were the same for all observers everywhere in the Universe. Second, that the speed of light in a **vacuum** is always constant. These ideas form part of Einstein's **theory of special relativity**.

The second idea, that the speed of light is always constant, seemed to go against common sense. Imagine a car travelling along a road at 60 km/h. If it passes a parked car, it passes it at 60 km/h. But if the other car is travelling at 40 km/h in the same direction then the first car passes the second one much more slowly. In fact it passes it at only 20 km/h. This is because the faster car has to catch up with the slower one. In the same way you can throw a ball faster by taking a run up before throwing it because the speed you are running at is added to the speed at which you throw the ball. These ideas were described by Newton's laws of motion.

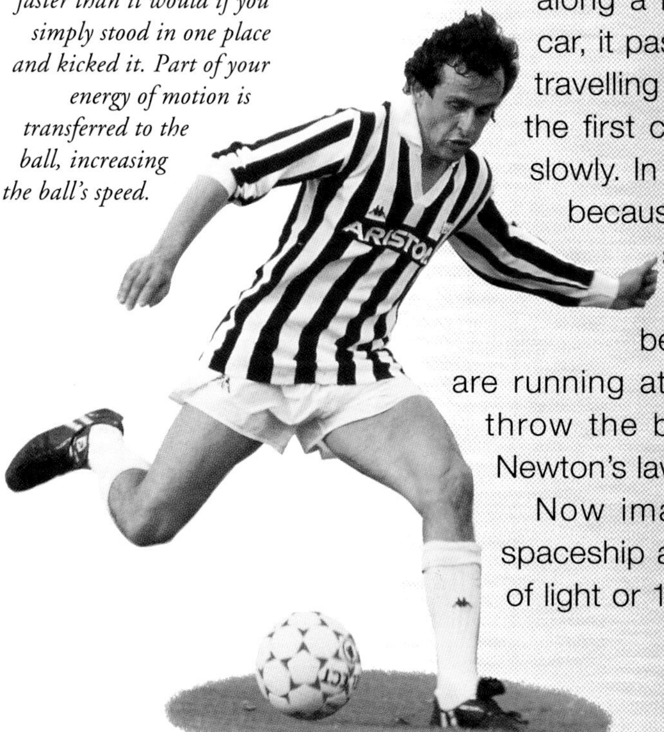

If you take a run up before kicking a ball, it will travel faster than it would if you simply stood in one place and kicked it. Part of your energy of motion is transferred to the ball, increasing the ball's speed.

Now imagine that a friend is travelling in a spaceship at a very high speed, say half the speed of light or 150,000 km/s. You are in a space station and, as she zooms past, you shine a beam of light towards her. You both measure the speed of the light beam as it passes her. What answers do you get?

Common sense says that you should reach different answers. You should measure the light's speed as 300,000 km/s as it travels away from you, but she should measure it as only 150,000 km/s because it has to catch up with her spaceship, which is travelling away from it. This isn't what happens. The light beam still passes her at 300,000 km/s. If you remember, the speed something travels at is the distance it travels divided by the time it takes to get there. If the speed of light in space is always the same, then time and space have to change.

No matter how fast a spaceship travels, a beam of light will always pass it at 300,000 km/s. Nothing can travel faster than light.

Strange things at high speeds

Einstein showed that unexpected things appear to happen to moving objects when they are measured by someone who is standing still in comparison. For one thing they seem to shrink. From the point of view of the object it doesn't really shrink. It only looks as though it does to someone watching it. As far as the fast-moving object is concerned, it is the person watching it who appears to shrink. This is surprisingly similar to one of the explanations that had been given for the result of Michelson and Morley's experiment regarding aether (see page 25). But Einstein did not know about their experiment which had been carried out 20 years earlier. He had worked this out for himself from his own theory and hadn't been influenced by the result of the Michelson and Morley experiment.

So how does time fit into this? Let's go back to the spaceship and space station again. For both you and your friend to reach the same answer for the speed of light, you have to reach agreement on the amount of time the light beam takes to reach her spaceship. What Einstein's theory does is to take away the idea of absolute time. There is no point in time called 'now' that we can all agree about. What happens is that you see time for your friend's spaceship running slow, which would allow the light beam to catch up with her and overtake her at the right speed. If her seconds are longer, the light beam can travel further and so reach the right place at the right time. But for her the opposite would seem to be true. Her clocks would still seem to keep the right time, but she would see your clocks running slow! Because your clocks seem to keep different times you can't agree when now is.

Atomic clocks work by measuring the vibrations of atoms of the element called caesium. The world's first caesium clock was built at the National Physical Laboratory in Teddington, near London. It was accurate to one second in every 10,000 years. Today's atomic clocks keep even better time – losing or gaining only one second in three million years! The clock above is in Germany.

These things are only obvious at very high speeds approaching that of light. In our everyday, slow-moving world the effects of motion are so tiny as to be unnoticeable. But they can be measured using highly-accurate **atomic clocks**. An atomic clock counts the vibrations of atoms. It can measure time to an accuracy of a millionth of a second a day. An atomic clock in an aeroplane will not agree with an atomic clock on the ground after a while. Because it has been travelling faster, time for the clock on the aeroplane has passed more slowly than for the clock on the ground. But the difference is only a few billionths of a second.

So to sum up, if you think your friend's spaceship is shorter than she thinks it is and she thinks your space station has shrunk, and if you think that her clocks are running slower than yours and she thinks your clocks are running slower than hers then the beam of light will pass her at the right speed!

Einstein thought that everyone was entitled to their point of view. It didn't matter if you thought she was speeding past you or if you were speeding past her. The results were the same whether it was her spaceship rushing away from your space station or whether her spaceship was standing still and the space station was moving away.

In fact, according to Einstein, as long as you were moving at a steady speed it would be impossible to tell which object was really moving and which was standing still. Your friend might see your space station flash by her window but how does she know that it's not the space station that is passing her? Referring to this notion in a light-hearted way Einstein is supposed to have turned to a fellow passenger on board a train and said: 'Excuse me, sir. Can you tell me what time Oxford stops at this train?'

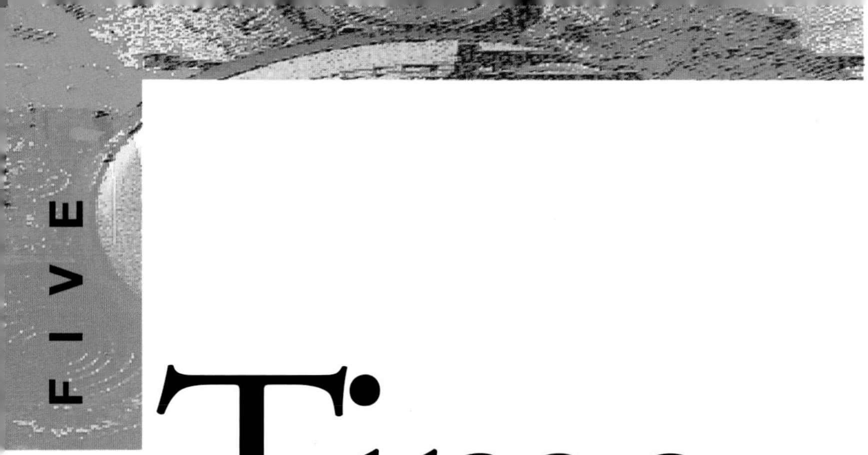

CHAPTER FIVE

Time and space

In 1908 Hermann Minkowski, who had been one of Einstein's teachers, gave a famous lecture which was inspired by the work of his former pupil. In the lecture he put forward the idea of space-time. He said that space and time could only exist together and that you couldn't have one without the other.

We have to think about both space and time to agree about what is happening. Let's go back for a moment to your friend in the superfast spaceship. You can't agree how much time has passed (because your clocks are running at different speeds), and you can't agree on how far your friend has travelled when the light beam passes her. What you have to do is take your time measurements and your space measurements (in other words, distance) together to give what is called a **space-time interval**.

If you do this you will find that you reach the same answer. As long as you know how fast she is travelling in relation to you, you will be able to work out when and where she is, and get the same answers as she does.

Space and time, then, are just different aspects of space-time. Your friend's spaceship only looks shorter to you because you are seeing it from a different point of view in space-time. To picture what this means try looking at a pencil with the tip pointing towards you. All you can see is a dot. Now turn the pencil so that

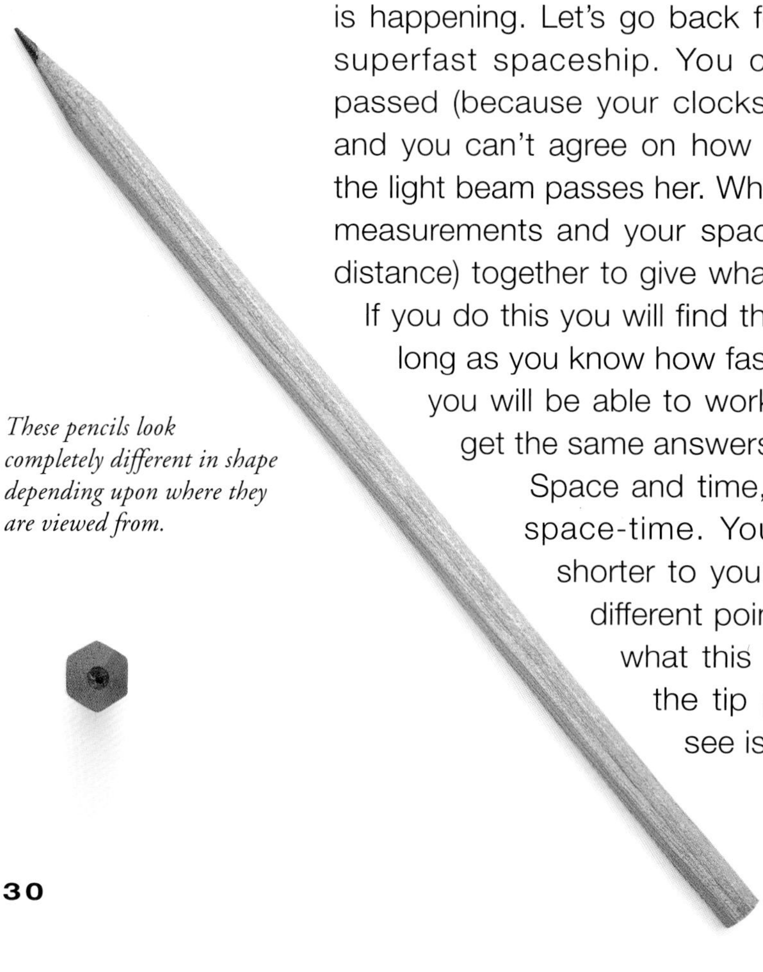

These pencils look completely different in shape depending upon where they are viewed from.

According to Einstein, time for the scientist who stays on Earth flows at a different rate from time for the astronaut in the high-speed spacecraft.

you can see its entire length. Now it looks like a line. So what is it – a dot or a line? It's both! Or neither. It's just a pencil from a different point of view. It stays the same, but the way you see it changes. The same thing applies to the spaceship – it looks different (and its clocks run at different speeds) when looked at from different positions in space-time.

General relativity

Einstein's special relativity theory didn't include gravity. It only concerned itself with objects that were moving at a steady speed – not getting faster or slowing down as they would if gravity was pulling on them. For the next few years he worked on his theory of general relativity that would include gravity.

Einstein's solution, published in 1916, was a surprising one. It involved space-time again. Einstein said that space-time is curved by the objects in it. The bigger the object, the more space-time is curved around it. According to Einstein, objects follow the shortest possible paths through curved space-time.

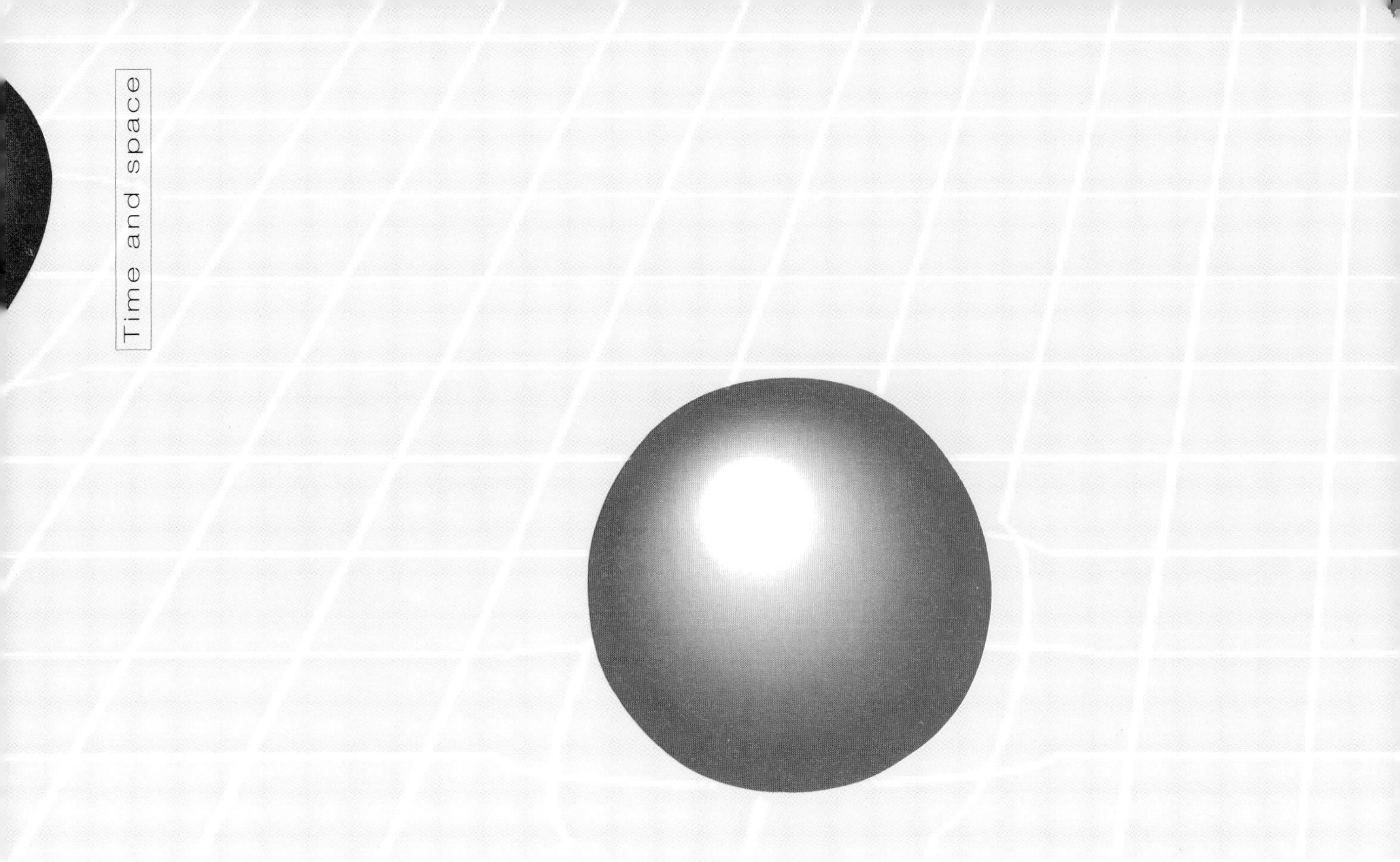

No one can really picture the way space-time is distorted by large objects, but you can get some idea by imagining that space is a flat sheet with objects such as stars and planets sitting on it and pulling it out of shape.

For instance, the Sun curves space-time so much that the Earth follows a circular path around it. If space-time were flat these paths would be straight lines. Einstein's idea of gravity was not some strange force that pulled objects towards each other. Instead it was the result of the curves in space-time. An apple doesn't fall from a tree because the Earth is pulling it. It is going down into the dent the Earth makes in space-time!

High time

One result of the curving of space-time is that time runs more slowly near a massive object. This means that a clock high above the Earth seems to run faster than a clock on the Earth's surface. The difference is very small. An atomic clock taken high up in a balloon will run a few billionths of a second an hour faster than one left on the ground. This is because the Earth doesn't curve space-time all that much! For everyday purposes, space-time can be thought of as flat. The ground looks flat when you walk on it, but we know that the Earth is curved. In the same way, the curves in space-time are really only important on a very large scale. Everybody still uses Newton's laws to work out how things will move. After all, Newton's answers are right 99.999 per cent of the time.

Like Galileo and Newton before him, Einstein changed the way we look at the Universe. It is no longer possible to think of space and time as being simply the background for everything to happen against. Space and time themselves are changed by what is happening in the Universe. And the way we see the Universe is changed by space-time.

The beginning of time

When Einstein used his ideas to try to work out how the whole Universe might work he came up with an idea that worried him. At that time people thought that the Universe had always been much the same as it is now and that it always would be. They thought that time had no beginning and no end. Everyone failed to see that gravity should pull everything in the Universe together.

Einstein was so sure that the Universe had to be unchanging that he added something called a **universal constant** to his theory. Later this became known as the **cosmological constant**. The cosmological constant acted like a mysterious sort of antigravity that more or less exactly balanced the force of gravity pulling everything together. The result was that the Universe stayed as it was. Later Einstein realized that he had made a mistake

Many people think that the Universe started out as a tiny point that expanded suddenly and very rapidly in a colossal cosmic event called the Big Bang. Over millions of years the energy and matter that were created in the Big Bang formed the Universe as we see it now.

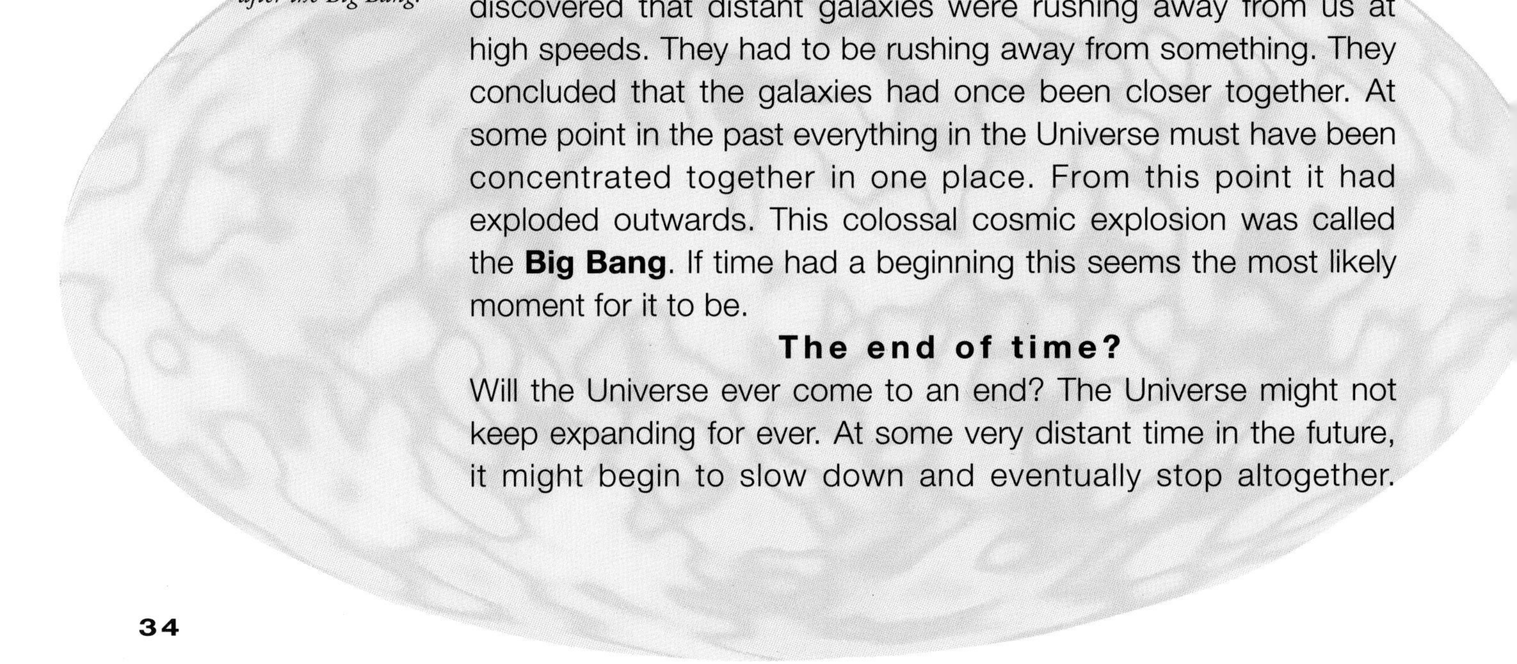

The Cosmic Background Explorer satellite (COBE) allowed scientists to build up this picture of the early Universe, just 300,000 years after the Big Bang.

and called this the biggest blunder of his life. Other people weren't so afraid of the idea of a changing Universe. Just over ten years after Einstein set out his ideas astronomers began to find the first evidence that the Universe was expanding. They discovered that distant galaxies were rushing away from us at high speeds. They had to be rushing away from something. They concluded that the galaxies had once been closer together. At some point in the past everything in the Universe must have been concentrated together in one place. From this point it had exploded outwards. This colossal cosmic explosion was called the **Big Bang**. If time had a beginning this seems the most likely moment for it to be.

The end of time?

Will the Universe ever come to an end? The Universe might not keep expanding for ever. At some very distant time in the future, it might begin to slow down and eventually stop altogether.

Then, under the pull of gravity, the Universe will start to collapse in on itself again.

After many millions of years, the Universe might contract back down to a single point, just as it was at the time of the Big Bang. Some people have called this the **Big Crunch**. What will happen then? Possibly the Universe will simply vanish. Or it might bounce back in another Big Bang and start all over again. It is possible that the Universe will just go on expanding and contracting for ever.

Would it be possible to build a time machine that could take someone back to see the Big Bang or forward to the Big Crunch? No, because at the moment of the Bang or Crunch time itself would not exist in any way that we can understand. So there would be nothing for the time machine to travel in. But what about a time machine that didn't go quite so far? Many scientists have explored ways of making time travel possible, but putting their ideas into practice would be extraordinarily difficult. Perhaps for a moment we should just let our imaginations go and try to picture what it would mean if we could travel, even a short way, through time.

Some people say that it would be impossible because it would create **paradoxes**. A paradox is a situation that does not make sense, or in some way goes against what we believe to be true or possible. The famous example is called the grandfather paradox. Suppose you went back in time to visit your grandfather before your father had been born. Unfortunately, your time machine lands on top of him and kills him. This means that your father will never be born, so you will never be born. But if you were never born, you could not go back and land on top of your grandfather! Which means that he would live, your father would be born and so would you. So you would go back in time to land on top of your grandfather. The problem repeats itself endlessly.

There may be a way round this problem. It involves the creation of new universes. Einstein's description of the Universe allows loops in space-time that lead into the past. There is also the strange possibility that these loops might lead into other universes that are only slightly different from our own. In one universe a time machine appears and squashes a man; but in the universe next door no time machine appears and the man goes on to have children and grandchildren. One of his grandchildren then builds a time machine and travels back along a loop to the first universe where it squashes the first man, who would have been his grandfather if he hadn't been killed.

However hard you try to create problems for space-time, it will always get the better of you simply by creating more universes.

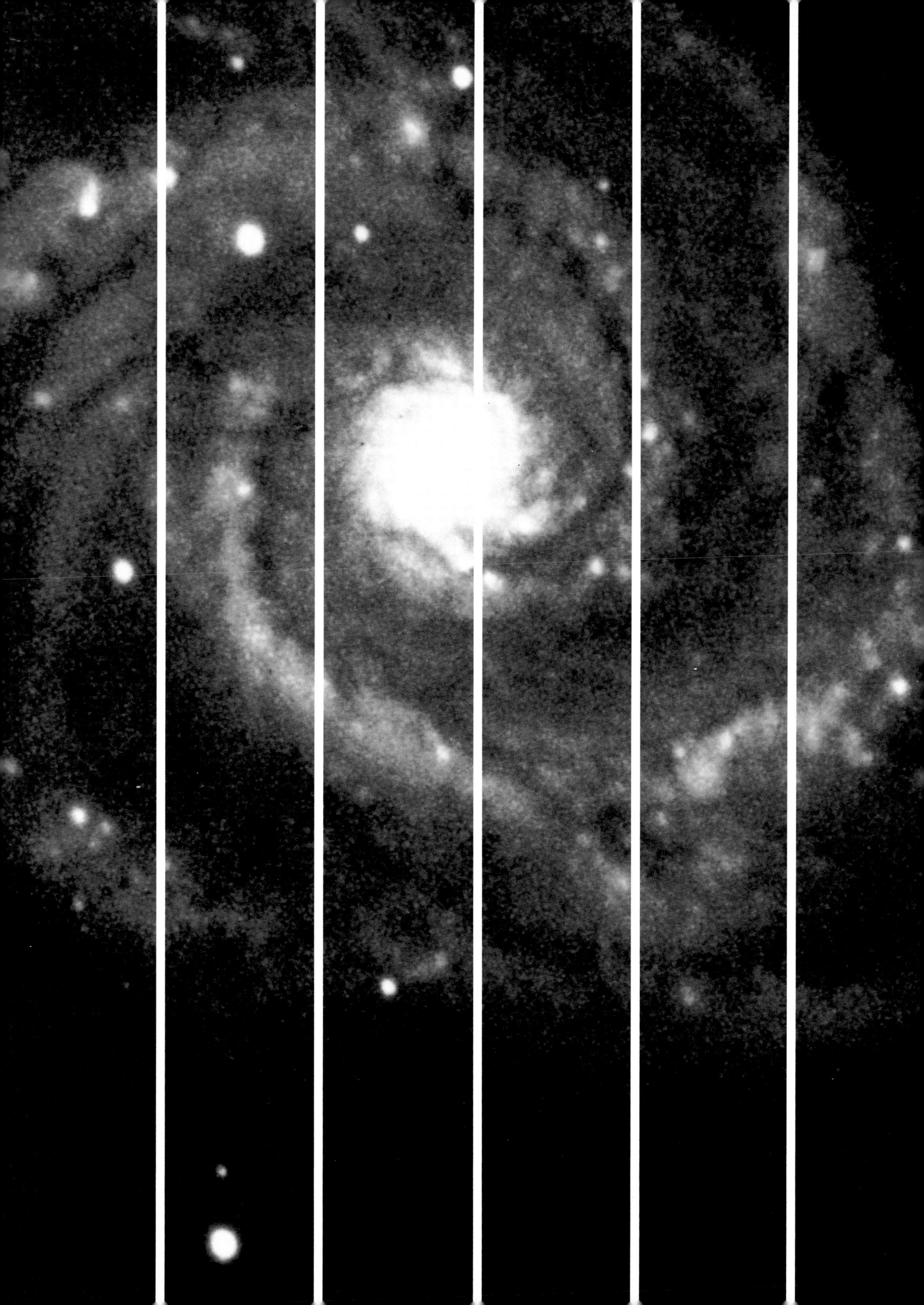

CHAPTER SIX

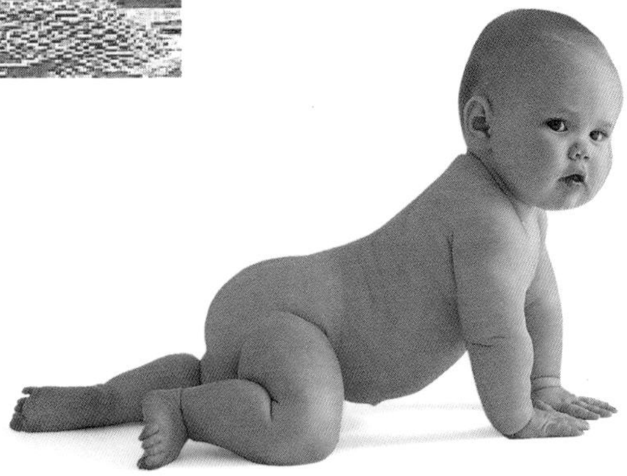

We're not getting any younger!

Why can we only go one way through time – into the future? If you see a photograph of yourself as a baby, you know that's how you used to be, not how you are going to be. And if you forget to send a friend a birthday card you can't turn back the clock to send it!

The idea of an **arrow of time** that points in only one direction – from the past into the future – was first introduced by the British astronomer Sir Arthur Eddington. The past is over and can't be changed, but it gives us some clues about what might happen in the future. In Chapter 3 we had a brief look at Isaac Newton's laws of motion.

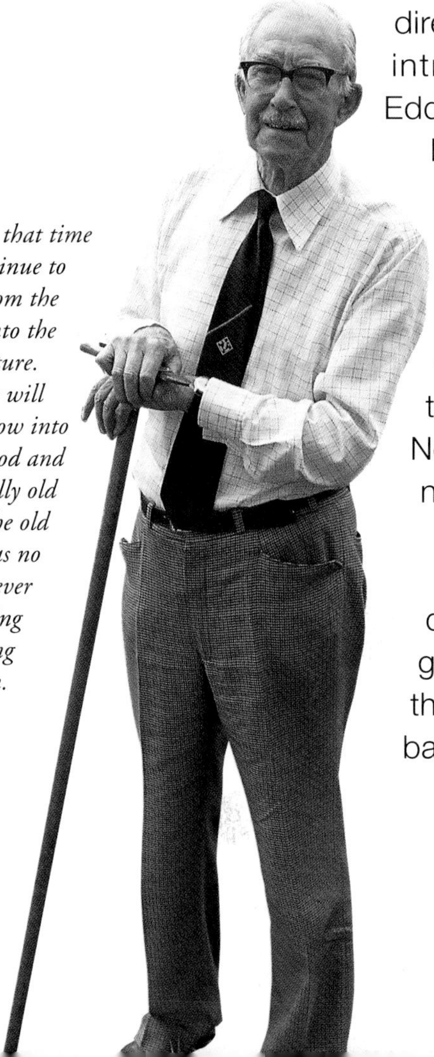

We expect that time will continue to flow from the past into the future. A baby will grow into adulthood and eventually old age, but the old man has no hope of ever growing young again.

Using Newton's laws

Newton's laws of motion allow people to work out the path a comet will follow around the Sun or the way a ball will bounce off a wall. Using Newton's laws, if you know how an object is moving now, you can work out how it was moving before and how it will be moving in the future.

Yet a funny thing about this theory is that it doesn't matter which time direction an object is going in. If we had a film of the comet going round the Sun, we wouldn't be able to tell if it was running backwards or forwards by applying Newton's laws.

And Newton couldn't tell us if I had bounced the ball off the wall for you to catch or if you had bounced it to me. Newton's laws are time-reversible – they work just as well in either direction.

If you saw a film of a cup falling from a table to break in pieces on the ground you would know that the film was running in the right direction. It would be very strange to see the broken cup rise into the air to reassemble itself on the table.

Yet, according to Newton's laws this would not be impossible. The reason you'll never see it happening is that it is very, very, improbable.

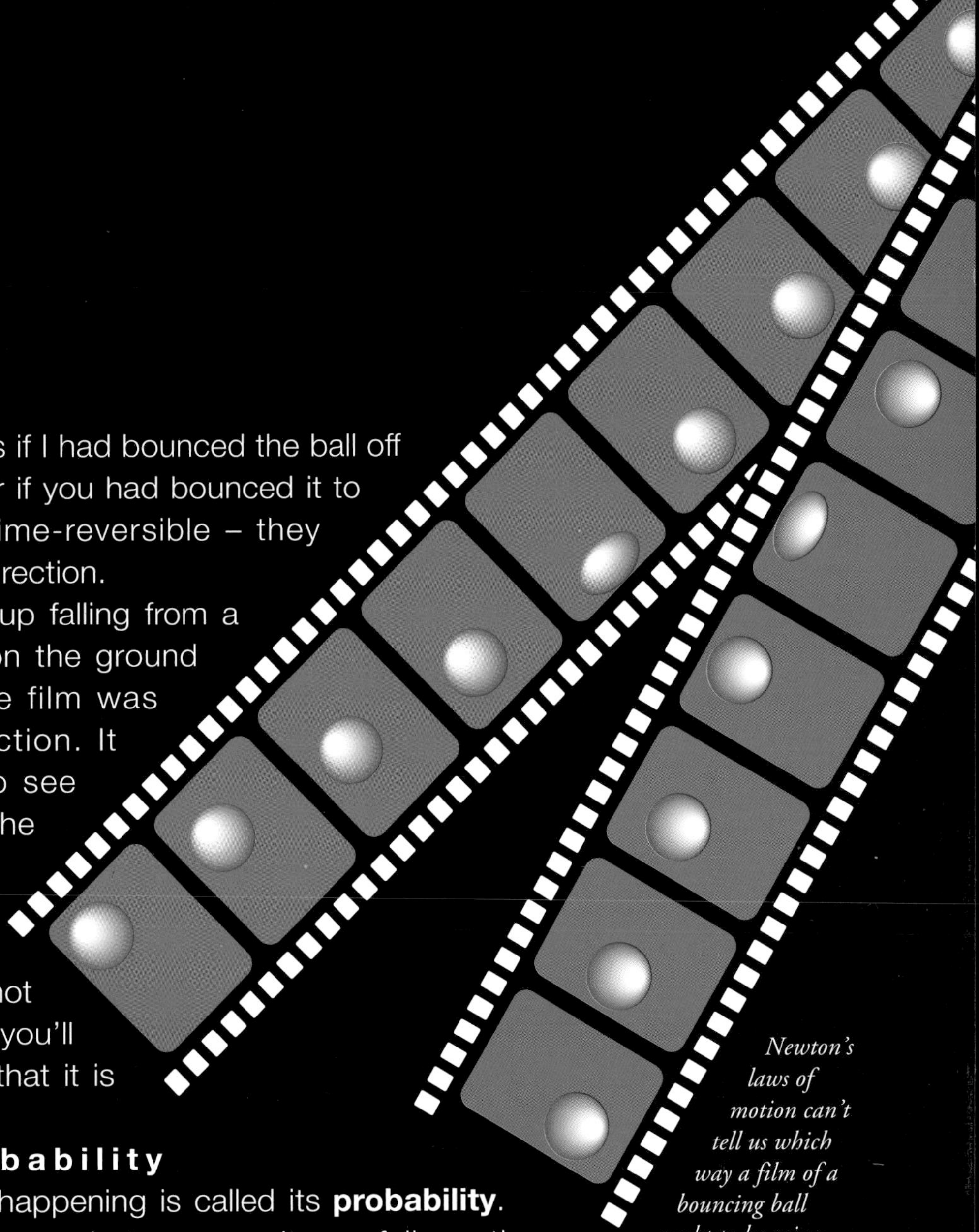

Newton's laws of motion can't tell us which way a film of a bouncing ball ought to be going. The rules work just as well whether they go forwards or backwards in time.

Probability

The chance of something happening is called its **probability**. If you toss a coin, there are only two ways it can fall, so the probability of it landing heads up is one chance in two. The probability of it landing tails up is the same.

A cup, like everything else, is made up of tiny particles, called **molecules**, all of which are moving around. There is absolutely nothing in Newton's laws to prevent all the molecules suddenly moving in the right direction so that the pieces of the cup fit back together again.

The point is that there are so many billions of molecules involved and so many directions they could move in. The probability of all the molecules moving the right way at the same time is so fantastically small that it just won't happen. And just in case you were wondering, there is nothing in Einstein's theories of relativity that wouldn't work backwards in time as well.

From order to disorder

Here, perhaps, is one reason why time only goes one way. It is highly unlikely that it should go in any other direction. The Universe seems to go from an ordered state into a disordered one. This increase in disorder is called **entropy**. It is the most likely way for events to run because there are so many more ways to be disordered than ordered. It takes energy to organize random objects into ordered ones. There is only a limited amount of energy available in the Universe. The entropy of the Universe is increasing and this gives us a very strong arrow of time.

You can only read and understand these words because they have been given a certain order that makes sense. The two paragraphs below contain exactly the same words and letters in the wrong order and positions.

and the letters words the contain paragraphs The makes order a been they words understand read can positions order the in and same exactly below two sense.that certain given have because these and only You.

sense certain understand read can positions paragraphs The makes given have because exactly below only You. letters words a and the, that these and the they in order words same and the contain been order

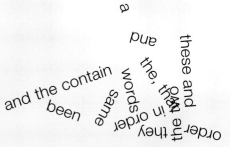

The entropy of a sentence that has meaning is lower than that of a sentence that makes no sense. To give my sentences meaning I use energy to think and to press the keys on my

keyboard. A lot of this energy is converted into heat and lost, so by writing this book I have increased the entropy of the Universe. We need order to give direction to time, whether it is the movement of the Earth around the Sun, or the vibrating atoms in an atomic clock. We look for the repeating patterns in the Universe that we can use to measure time.

Thunder and lightning reveal the enormous energy latent in the Universe. This energy, according to the Big Bang theory, was all released at one point and it is endlessly changing.

It wouldn't make sense to talk about an arrow of time if all the particles in the Universe were evenly spaced and moving around randomly. There would still be time, since things would still be happening, but there would be no way of telling in which direction the arrow was pointing. Why should there be any order in the Universe at all? There was one, possibly unique, event that gave time its direction. We came across it in the last chapter – the Big Bang.

Exploding into the future

When the Universe began with the Big Bang it was in a highly ordered state. Everything in it was concentrated into a single point. For some reason (we don't know why) this point expanded at a colossal rate. It increased in size a million million million million million times in a fraction of a second.

The same **cosmic processes** that powered this fantastic inflation also created huge amounts of energy – all the energy the Universe would ever have. When the rate of expansion slowed down the energy changed into particles and **radiation**, in the same way as steam can cool into water and ice. Before this happened the Universe had been featureless, now suddenly it was filled with particles. It had become disordered. Here and there a few particles moved together randomly and the tiny irregularities they made in space-time drew other particles in.

This is how the stars began to form. The entropy arrow of time was pointing towards the future.

Contracting into the past?

What happens if the Universe doesn't go on expanding for ever? Suppose one day in the far, far distant future the expansion of the Universe slowed down and stopped altogether and the force of gravity began very slowly to bring everything back together again. If the Universe was going backwards would time run in reverse as well? The answer is that it almost certainly wouldn't. If it did, then right at the moment the Universe started to collapse again, time would be going forwards and backwards at the same instant, which is hard to imagine!

What would life be like in a backward-time universe? Would birds fly backwards? Would you spit out bits of fruit that would join up to make a whole apple in your hand? One scientist suggested that if time ran backwards, light would shine from people's eyes to illuminate the stars. It is much more

Professor Stephen Hawking, whose ideas on the nature of time have won great respect.

likely that time won't go into reverse. Entropy will still be increasing as the Universe contracts and the arrow of time will still point forward. Professor Stephen Hawking thinks that we couldn't exist without the entropy arrow. People, he says, eat food, which is an ordered form of energy, and convert some of it into heat, which is disordered energy. If the arrow of time pointed backwards we wouldn't be here to know about it.

Time moves on

So what is time? Even Albert Einstein, who did so much to change our ideas about time, didn't attempt to solve the problem of why time only goes forward. We've discovered that in the everyday world we can say that something happens at a certain time. But we can only say what happens by referring to something else, whether it is the rising of the Sun or the ticking of an atomic clock. Einstein showed that there couldn't be any ultimate timekeeper against which all the clocks and watches of the Universe could be set. Time depends on where you are and runs faster or slower according to your situation.

Understanding time

The key to understanding the Universe is probably understanding time. Everything takes time. Nothing happens without it. We feel time passing. We can remember the past, but we have no knowledge of the future. We are always balanced at a single moment we call the present with time past behind us and time future to come.

We are only here for a very short span of time in the life of the Universe. The history of the human race takes up only the most fleeting of moments when set against the huge gulfs of time that have passed since the beginning of the Universe. Yet people are trying to look into the secrets of time itself, to find out how it works and what it is. Will we ever find an answer to the puzzle?

Time will tell.

Glossary

Absolute position *Isaac Newton believed that it was possible, in theory, to give the position of any object in the Universe without reference to any other object. This was its absolute position in absolute space.*

Absolute space *The background of the Universe against which everything was placed, according to Isaac Newton.*

Absolute time *Isaac Newton's belief that time passes at the same rate throughout the Universe so that it is always the same time everywhere.*

Aether *An invisible substance which scientists thought carried light waves and other forms of radiation across space. We now know that aether does not exist and that light can travel through empty space.*

Arrow of time *The idea of time's arrow pointing in one direction only, from the past into the future. The phrase was first used by Sir Arthur Eddington in 1927.*

Atomic clock *A clock that measures time by counting the number of vibrations per second in certain atoms.*

Big Bang *The name given to the theory that all of the matter and energy in the Universe originated in a sudden explosion outwards from a single point around 15 billion years ago.*

Big Crunch *The name given to the theory that in the far future all the matter and energy in the Universe will collapse back into a single point, similar to the one from which it all started in the Big Bang.*

Chandelier *A branched hanging support for lights. Observing a swinging chandelier in Pisa is supposed to have sparked Galileo's studies of pendulums.*

Common time *The name Isaac Newton gave to the everyday time that we follow in our daily lives to distinguish it from his universal absolute time.*

Constant *In physics a constant is a quantity that does not vary but is carried unchanged from one equation to another. The speed of light in free space is an example of a universal constant; it is the same wherever it is measured in the Universe. Whenever a calculation is made involving the speed of light the figure used is always the same.*

Cosmic processes *Processes that take place in the whole Universe.*

Cosmological constant *A constant introduced into his equations by Albert Einstein to balance the force of gravity and ensure that the Universe would neither expand nor contract. He later called this the biggest blunder of his life.*

Entropy *A measure of disorder, or the unavailability of energy in a system to do work. Every time work is done, some energy is lost as heat and is no longer available to do more work. This results in an increase in entropy.*

Gnomon *The upright part of a sundial that casts the shadow on the face of the dial.*

Gravitational force *The force that acts between any two objects in the Universe, attracting them to each other.*

Gregorian calendar *A revised calendar introduced by Pope Gregory in 1582 to correct inaccuracies that had crept in since Julius Caesar had introduced his calendar in 45 BC. The Gregorian calendar is still used today.*

Leap year *A year in which an extra day is added to the month of February, making it 29 days long rather than 28. This is done because a year cannot be divided into an equal number of days, as it is roughly 365.25 long. All the quarter days are added every fourth year at the end of February.*

Lunar month *The time between one new moon and the next. It is equal to 29 days, 12 hours, and 44 minutes.*

Master cycle *A cycle, or regularly occurring series of events, against which others can be measured. For example, we might choose the day as our master cycle. It can be split into smaller parts, hours, or multiplied to give a longer length, a year. In this case the master cycle is the day, the time between one sunrise and the next. If we measure the length of an hour and a year in terms of day length, an hour is a 24th of a day and a year is 365 days.*

Molecules *These are the smallest parts of a chemical compound that can take part in chemical reactions. Molecules are groups of atoms bound together. These atoms can be of the same or different kinds. For example, a molecule of oxygen consists of two oxygen atoms bound together; a molecule of carbon dioxide gas consists of two oxygen atoms and one carbon atom.*

Patterns of interference *Patterns of interference are set up when two or more waves pass through each other. Where the waves cross they add their energy together. If the crest of one wave coincides with the trough of another they cancel each other out. If two crests coincide they create a wave that is twice as big. These patterns show us where the waves are adding energy and where they are cancelling each other out. In the case of light, dark areas in the interference patterns show us where the waves are cancelling each other out.*

Probability *The chance of something happening is called its probability. Probabilities are always less than 1. For example, if you toss a coin the probability of it coming up heads is 0.5, or one chance in two; if you roll a die the probability of any particular number coming up is 0.166, or one chance in six. Anything that is absolutely certain to happen has a probability of 1, but then nothing in science is absolutely certain!*

Radiation *Radiation includes electromagnetic waves, such as light, X-rays, and gamma rays, as well as high-energy atomic particles.*

Sidereal day *The time it takes for the Earth to rotate once on its axis, measured by observing the positions of the stars. It is 4.09 minutes shorter than a solar day.* Sidereal *comes from a Latin word meaning star.*

Solar day *The time it takes for the Earth to rotate once on its axis. It is measured as the time between two successive returns of the Sun to its highest point in the sky each day.*

Solar year *Throughout the year the Sun rises in slightly different places each day. A solar year is the time it takes for the Sun to return again to rise in the same place. It is the time it takes for the Earth to go around the Sun once and is equal to 365.242 solar days.*

Space-time interval *In Albert Einstein's relativity theories, space and time are linked together, so that an object is given a position in time as well as in space. A space-time interval is the separation between two events in space-time. For example, the space-time interval between the birth of Albert Einstein (in Ulm, Germany, 14 March 1879) and his death (in Princeton, USA, 18 April 1955) is roughly 700 kilometres and 76 years.*

Special relativity *A theory put forward by Albert Einstein in 1905 in which he began by assuming that the set of rules that governs the workings of the Universe are the same for all observers everywhere who are stationary or moving at a constant speed, and that the speed of light is a* ***constant****. One of the conclusions of this theory was that energy and mass are equivalent, linked by Einstein's famous equation* $E = mc^2$*, where* E *= energy,* m *= mass, and* c *= the speed of light, a universal constant. The faster something goes the more energy it has and so the greater its mass becomes.*

Universal constant *see* **constant**

Vacuum *A space in which there are relatively few molecules or atoms. A perfect vacuum, in which there is nothing at all, does not exist. Even in deep space between the stars there are still, on average, a million hydrogen atoms per cubic metre.*

Water clock *A clock that measures time by the steady dripping of water.*

Index

Numbers in bold indicate illustrations